The Gardening Book

Jane Bull

A Dorling Kindersley Book

A Penguin Company
LONDON, NEW YORK, MUNICH,
MELBOURNE, AND DELHI

DESIGN • Jane Bull
EDITOR • Penny Arlon
PHOTOGRAPHY • Andy Crawford
DESIGN ASSISTANCE • Abbie Collinson

MANAGING EDITOR • Sue Leonard
MANAGING ART EDITOR • Cathy Chesson
PRODUCTION • Shivani Pandey
DTP DESIGNER • Almudena Díaz

For Charlotte, Billy, and James

First published in Great Britain in 2003 by
Dorling Kindersley Limited
80 Strand,
London WC2R 0RL

4 6 8 10 9 7 5 3

A CIP catalogue record for this book
is available from the British Library

ISBN: 978-0-7513-6473-6

Colour reproduction by
GRB Editrice S.r.l., Verona, Italy
Printed and bound in China by Toppan

See our complete
catalogue at
www.dk.com

Help your plants to grow big and strong

What's growing in the garden?

Plant some seeds...

...and watch them grow!

Get Growing - Gardening with or

Here are the tools and materials you

will need to get you started.

Look out for me!
I tell you when
to plant your seeds

Which soil to use?

MULTI-PURPOSE COMPOST
You will need this for growing everything from seeds to big plants.

MULTI-PURPOSE
COMPOST

GRAVEL

PEBBLES

Always add gravel or pebbles to the bottom of a plant pot before you fill it with compost. This helps the water to drain away so that the roots of your plants don't get too soggy.

What to grow?

SEEDS • Buy your seeds in packets. If you want to know details about the plant read the packet carefully (see page 46). Alternatively, you can try growing plants by taking the seeds from the vegetables, or fruit that you eat or from plants in the garden.

PLANTS •
Fully grown
plants give
you an instant
garden. It is best
to buy small, young
plants, like the ones in
this book, as they don't
take up too much space. Each
one will come with a label. Read
it carefully to see which plants you
are buying and what they need in
order to grow well.

Sunflower seeds

Which pots?

You can use all sorts of containers to grow your plants in. Most of the projects in this book use plant pots that are easy to buy and come in plastic or terracotta. They are equally as good as each other and can both be decorated.

PLASTIC POT

TERRACOTTA POT

DRIP TRAY

Drip trays can be plastic or terracotta. They are handy because you can water the plants from the base instead of at the top.

RECYCLED POTS – small containers, such as yoghurt pots and fruit and vegetable trays, are ideal for sowing seeds.

Watering and feeding

WATERING • Water plants well when you first plant or re-pot them. Then check them each day. If it's sunny they might need watering every day. Big plants, such as marrows, get very thirsty.

Spraying small seedlings and plants is often enough to keep them moist.

WATERING CAN

WATER SPRAYER

FEEDING • Plants, such as squash and tomato plants, need something extra in their water. Buy some plant food/liquid fertilizer and mix it into the water. You are then feeding them at the same time as giving them a drink.

Look out for me!
I remind you when to water

What else is needed?

- Plant labels, pencil or a waterproof pen – always remember to label your plants and seedlings.
- Plastic bags for keeping seeds warm and moist.
- Plant ties and stick canes to support tall plants.

REMEMBER!

Plants must have two important things to help them grow:

WATER
and
LIGHT

Grow these any time of year

Pocket Plots

Grow a miniature garden that fits in the palm of your hand.

Take the lid off a pot or jar and sow some seeds in it.
Create a tiny home for all your tiny toys.

❀ What's in your pocket plot?

Mustard and cress seeds are the best to use. They are super-speedy growers
and will sprout anywhere as long as they are kept damp. Keep the plots
watered and you'll even be able to pick some stalks to put in a sandwich.

Prepare your plot

Take a clean lid

Lay down some damp tissue

Use a mixture of mustard and cress seeds.

Only put the seeds in the areas that you want covered.

Sprinkle on the seeds

Take a peek every day. When you can see the little shoots, take the cover off.

Keep the tissue damp.

Cover them up

If you water your pocket plot regularly, it will last longer.

Let them grow

Lost World

Grow this any time of year

Discover a place that time has forgotten, where creatures roam freely amongst the lush foliage. But don't hang around or you might be spotted!

Take a bird's eye view of the forgotten land

❀ Bring it to life

In the forgotten world anything goes – from the smallest man to the biggest animal. Watch the tiny people hide under the plants, threatened by the terrifying monsters. Create a world of your own and live your own wild adventures.

Quick, find a bushy plant to hide behind!

Look, the rescue helicopter is here. Phew! If it can land they will all be safe.

Please! Create a world for me

Try to imagine what type of lush kingdom dinosaurs would like to roam around in. Use small houseplants to create your prehistoric landscape.

Small, young houseplants are ideal – look out for things like ferns and palms.

Prepare the land

This tray is about 40 cm (16 in) x 25 cm (10 in) and about 10 cm (4 in) deep.

Spread a layer of gravel, about 2 cm ($^3/4$ in) deep, over the bottom of the tray.

Cover the gravel with a thick layer of compost, almost to the top.

Work out how you are going to design your world by moving the plants around while they are in their pots.

Plant the landscape

Slip the plant out of the pot
Hold it lightly in your fingers

Water the plants to help them settle in.

Make a hole in the soil – about the size of the plant's roots. Pop the plant into the hole and lightly press it down. Place some soil around the edges to level it out.

Now bring us to life

Use big stones or small pebbles to add to your landscape.

❀ Keeping alive

Remember to water your world about once a week. Add some plant food to the water every so often to keep the plants healthy. Your world should stay indoors out of direct sunlight – although of course you can take it outside to play with. If your plants grow too big, you may have to replant them, or simply make a bigger kingdom.

Spraying your plants every two days will keep them fresh

Use gravel to make a winding track.

11

Bonsai Fakes

It may look like a bonsai

tree, but it's really just a baby tree.

Make this anytime

REAL BONSAI

What's a real bonsai?

The word "bonsai" is Chinese and means "tree in a pot". A bonsai is a real tree that is grown in a pot from a seed, and then cut and pruned to keep it tiny. Bonsai trees are seasonal, just like big trees, and can live for hundreds of years.

Make a meadow by planting moss at the base.

The moss looks just like a grassy meadow. Let's take a rest

FAKE BONSAI

What makes a fake?

Bonsai trees are pretty difficult to grow so the best thing to do is find a fake. Dwarf conifers are small trees that are used in rockeries. They only grow to about 60 cm (2 ft) and that takes about five years, so they are perfect to grow in a pot.

How to grow a fake

Select the tiniest conifer you can find.

- Put a layer of gravel then a layer of compost in a pot.
- Remove the tree from its pot and pop it in.
- Fill the space around the plant with extra compost.
- Give it some water and keep it outside or inside.
- Re-pot the bonsai when it gets too big.

Create a tiny playground.

FAKE BONSAI

I can't believe it's not a real bonsai

You could also sprinkle gravel around the tree.

FAKE BONSAI

REAL BONSAI

Grass People

Grow then groom these grassy heads. Who wants a haircut?

Tie a knot in one end and turn it inside out.

Pinch out a nose and tie it with an elastic band.

Soak it in a bowl of water until it is completely wet through.

Cut out a 30 cm (12 in) strip from some nylon tights.

Place a handful of grass seed inside.

Fill the rest of it up with sawdust and tie a knot in the top.

Keep your hair on!

Once you have prepared your head, put it upright in a dish. Make sure the nose is in the right place – remember, grass always grows upwards. Sprinkle it with water every day, and when the hair has gone wild, give it a haircut.

The grass seeds are now at the top.

Give it a face. Stick on eyes and other features.

Bad hair day?

Grow the grass in a pot instead. Sow the seed and in a few weeks the grassy hair will grow. But if you don't take control, it'll grow and grow and grow!

Give me a trim!

Place some gravel at the bottom of the pot, fill it with soil, and sprinkle a handful of seeds on the surface. Keep it damp and in a light place, and whatever you do, don't let it get out of control!

Sow these seeds in spring

A Sprinkle of Magic Seeds

Each tiny seed holds the magic to make your flowers grow.

Look closer!
This isn't dust,
it's a poppy seed

16

Cosmos

Cornflower

Marigold

Cornflower

Scabious

Zinnia

Poppy

Hey presto! An explosion of beautiful flowers

❀ **It's an annual event.** These seeds will grow into plants called annuals. This means that they complete their life cycle in one year – growing from seed, flowering, setting seed, and dying. Then their seeds start the cycle again.

Marigold

Aster

Scabious

Marigold

Poppy

Magic in a Pot

You don't need a huge space to grow a wild garden. Let the plants go wild in a flower pot.

Buy a seed packet that contains seeds for growing annuals.

How to grow your magic seeds

- Place some pebbles at the bottom of a 22 cm (9 in) plant pot.
- Fill the pot to the brim with potting compost.
- Sprinkle about 20 seeds on the top, cover them with a bit of compost, and water them. Leave the pot in a warm, light place.
- After a couple of weeks seedlings will begin to show.
- If the pot is looking crowded pull out some seedlings to make room for the strong ones to push through. Put the pot outside at this stage.
- Water the plants regularly and watch them grow.

Sprinkle about 20 seeds

22 cm (9 in) pot

The pebbles stop the soil from getting too soggy.

Cover the seeds with a sprinkle of compost.

If you need to, pull out some seedlings to allow more room.

When you have good growth from your seedlings, you can put the pot outside.

Try a whole bucket full of magic

Ah! Home at last!

✿ Magic care
• When your plants start growing, keep the pot outside in a sheltered, sunny spot.
• Water the pot enough to stop it from drying out.

Collecting seeds
As your flowers fade they will produce seeds. When they look quite dry, collect them and try sowing them next spring. Dry the seeds by placing them on kitchen paper. Keep them in an envelope labelled with the name and date. Store in a dry place.

Marigold seeds

When they are ready the seeds will come away easily.

Poppy seeds

The Sunflower Circle

Which came first, the flower or the seed?

Start your circle in the spring

Plant a *seed*

Help it grow

Feed the plant

See the flower appear

Let it fade

Collect the seeds

Now join the sunflower circle! Buy some seeds and grow a sunflower, collect the seeds when the flower fades, and off you go again.

Join the Sunflower Circle

In springtime buy some sunflower seeds or simply collect them from a friend's flower.

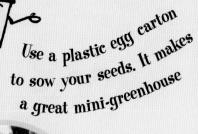

Use a plastic egg carton to sow your seeds. It makes a great mini-greenhouse

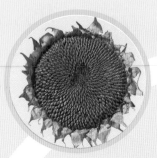

Around you go

1. Fill the cups of an egg carton with compost. Push one seed into each cup so that it is covered by the soil. Water to make the soil damp.
2. Place the carton in a light place and keep moist. Shoots will appear after about a week.
3. When two leaves have appeared you will have to move the plant to a pot. Fill a large pot with compost. Pop in your seedling and water it.
4. Let the seedling grow. Keep it watered, fed, and in good light.
5. When the sunflower gets very tall stick a long cane into the pot and tie the stalk to it to keep it upright.
6. Collect the seeds when the flower head has completely dried out.

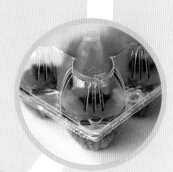

How tall will it grow?

If you buy the sunflower seeds in a packet, check to see how tall they will grow. Some grow taller than others. Watch out, you could find yourself with a sunflower 3 m (10 ft) in height!

To keep your plant upright stick a cane in the pot and tie them together with string.

Wild attraction

Keep an eye on your sunflowers, they will attract all sorts of wildlife. Look out for butterflies and bees when the flower is in full bloom, then as it fades cheeky birds may use it as a snack bar and nibble the seeds.

Feed the birds

Seed collection

The seeds will fall out easily when the flower has dried up. Leave the seeds in the sun to dry; then put them into envelopes.

Name and date the packet.

Have some sunflower fun

Who has the tallest sunflower?

How do they measure up? Get together and have a competition.

Buckets of fun

If you grow a dwarf sunflower, you can plant it straight into a big bucket or pot. Taller flowers, however, will grow stronger if you start them off in smaller pots.

Draw a face on your pebble.

My sunflower is the one with the ladybird

Paint some pebbles and use them as markers. Lay them on top of the pot.
See page 41 for pebble painting.

What a Squash!
Meet the squash family, here are a few you may recognize.

Sow seeds in **late spring**

Big stripy Ma marrow

Plump Pa pumpkin

Big cousin courgette...

...and junior courgette

Look out! Sometimes courgettes are called zucchinis.

Ready or not

When courgettes are big enough, cut them off the plant and cook them, or just let them get bigger and bigger!

24

Take a look at these fine young pumpkins

Green giant

Watch and be amazed as your seed grows and grows and grows from a tiny seedling into a massive plant, with flowers that yell...

"LOOK AT ME!"

Follow the pumpkin trail from tip to root

LOOK at ME!

Can you guess what's growing in this pot?

Get ready for Halloween

Even small pumpkins are scary

Squash in a Pot
Start off your squash in a small pot and as it gets more squashed as it grows, move it to a bigger pot.

After about six weeks *they are* *ready to pick*

Start in spring
Harvest in the summer

As the plant grows it moves up a pot size

GRAVEL OR PEBBLES

POTTING COMPOST

2.5 CM (1 IN) POT

7.5 CM (3 IN) POT

15 CM (6 IN) POT

23 CM (9 IN) POT

Seeds – use marrow, courgette, or pumpkin

Scary little pumpkins
Pumpkin plants can take up more space than marrow or courgette plants because they spread themselves out. Choose a small or dwarf variety that are easier to grow. Remember, small Jack-o'lanterns are just as scary.

Watch it grow

When you can see a sprout, remove the bag.

After two weeks the plant should be this big.

I'm three weeks old

2.5 cm (1 in) pot

Push the seed in 1 cm (¹/₃ in) deep.

Wrap the pot in a plastic bag to keep in heat and moisture.

Sometimes the seed is still on the bud.

7.5 cm (3 in) pot

✿ Growing tips

From seed • It is best to plant the seeds in the spring. Make sure you push the seed about 2.5 cm (1 in) beneath the surface of the compost. Water it regularly and place it on a light, warm windowsill.

Moving to bigger pots • As the seedlings get bigger, you must move them to bigger pots otherwise the roots cannot grow properly.

Watering and feeding • Keep the soil moist at all times, but be careful not to over water it. Add plant food to the water. The plant will need it when it is going to produce fruit.

This plant looks very hairy from here

The leaves keep growing

then the flower stalks appear

15 cm (6 in) pot

Don't squash the squash

Make regular checks on your squash. Take it out of the pot and if the roots look too crowded, move it to a bigger one.

Support the plant between your fingers.

Hold on to the base of the pot.

Look at the roots, if they need more room it's time to move on

Turn the pot over.

Let the plant slip out of the pot.

Prepare the next pot with a layer of pebbles then compost. Place the plant in the centre and fill round it with soil. Press it down and give it some water.

The growing continues . . .

... and will go on and on and on! When you have picked your squash, you have truly succeeded. Cook up a meal with your home-grown veggies.

Once the plant has a few leaves, it can then be taken outside. Make sure it is in a warm spot, away from the wind.

Sweet Tomatoes

Start sowing seeds in early spring

Tiny tomatoes. Big taste!

Look for small varieties like cherry tomatoes. They not only taste the sweetest, but the plants only grow to about 40 cm (16 in) high. This means that you can grow them in small pots and you won't need canes to support them.

The **tiny, sweet** tomatoes are the best for tasty, bite-sized snacks.

From pip to plant

1. Fill a small pot with compost. Push a seed into the centre, just below the soil.
2. Place the pot on a windowsill and give it some water. Check it everyday to make sure it is moist. In about a week it should start to sprout.
3. When it has outgrown the pot, carefully move it to a bigger one.
4. Feed it with plant food, water it regularly, and wait for flowers to appear.

Cover the seed with compost.

At two weeks

At four weeks

28

Keep me fed and watered

Get up close to your plants

Can you see their hairy stalks?

When you see flowers, you'll know the fruit is on its way. The flowers disappear and the baby fruit grows in their place. After a few weeks the fruit will ripen.

Tomato tips

Planting pips

Cut open a tomato and scoop out the little pips. Dry them with kitchen paper, then try planting them instead of the packet ones. What do you think will happen?

Packet tomato seeds

Tomato snacks

Wait until the tomatoes are completely red, then pick them and eat them as snacks. You will find that your home-grown tomatoes are the tastiest of all.

Ladybird friends

If you see a ladybird on your tomato plant, don't move it. They are your friends. Ladybirds eat the greenfly that want a bite of your tomatoes.

Sage Parsley

Lemon balm

Apple mint

Come to your Senses Garden

Curry plant

Scratch and sniff your way around the herb plants.

Marjoram

Chives

PLEASE!
Touch the plants

Good scents

Every herb plant has its own special smell. Rub the leaves between your fingers and thumb then sniff them. Can you tell which herb it is just by the smell?

Sight

Taste

Touch

Sound

Smell

Carry around good herb smells

Look at all the plant colours and shapes

Silver, purple, orange, green

Feathery, wispy, furry, wrinkly

These plant labels are made from Ping-Pong balls on sticks.

What's the Sense?

Some sensible ways

to make the most of your senses.

Sight

Look out

Decorate your garden with painted pots and plant labels to show what's growing where. See page 41.

Keep an eye on the garden

Touchy-feely

The more you touch herbs, the more they give off their aroma. Rub the plants between your fingers and smell them.

Soft and furry

Touch

Good taste

Herbs can help to make food taste even better. Chop up the leaves or use them whole.

Taste

Mix together chopped chives and cream cheese.

Try it with a baked potato.

Mint

Coriander

Thyme

Rosemary

Parsley

Sage

A bunch of herb leaves can be added to soups and stews while they are cooking to add extra taste.

Stop! Listen

Stop for a moment. Stay very still. What do you hear? Are there birds singing, bees buzzing, or leaves rustling? Enjoy the sounds your garden makes.

Sound

Smelly bundles

Smell

Tie up some herbs in a bundle and pop them in a drawer or even your pocket. Lavender is great to use as it has a lovely, strong smell.

Catnip sock toy

Cats go wild over catnip.

Fresh herbs all wrapped up.

Freshen up the dog's basket

Listen to the wind
with a wind chime

How to Come to Your Senses

Find out what to use your herbs for, and start your very own herb garden.

Plant pot windchime

Terracotta pots are the best things for creating a soothing jingle-jangle in your windy garden.

TERRACOTTA POT   STRING   PLASTIC LID   BEADS, ETC

Tie the string to a branch in the garden.

Knot the strings together.

Leave part of the string hanging down below the pot.

Pull some string through the hole in the pot. Attach a bead to the end that will sit under the hole.

Tie the four pieces of string to the main piece.

Ask an adult to help you cut a large hole in the centre of the plastic lid, then eight smaller ones around the edge. Tie a piece of string to every other hole.

Attach a length of string to each hole and hang a pebble, shell, or bead from each one.

Tie a pebble onto the string hanging through the centre, to weigh it down.

Self-contained herb garden

Spring and summertime

Magic up an instant herb garden in a pot. Choose herbs for their smell, colour, or taste. Decorate the container with a design that suits your pot garden. Keep it watered and in a warm, sheltered spot.

These are small plants. After a year they may need to move to a bigger pot.

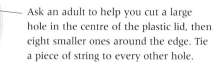

Parsley

Lemon balm

Sage

Marjoram

Dill

Find a pot large enough to take three to five plants.

Layer of pebbles

Handy herbs

They may be small but herbs have the most amazing number of different uses. From food flavourings and scents to dyes and healing remedies, herbs are essential to our lives.

Refreshing mints

There are more flavours of mint than you could ever imagine – peppermint, spearmint, and lemon mint, to name a few. Mint herbs are used in many things, such as chewing gum, toothpaste, and flavoured teas. Can you think of any more?

Sweet smells

Herbs such as lavender and camomile have a lovely strong smell. These are great herbs for your herb bags or simply to put in a drawer to make clothes smell nice.

Savoury tastes

Rosemary, thyme, parsley, sage, and oregano are herbs that are most commonly used to enhance savoury foods, such as sausages, fish, or vegetables. They all have very different tastes.

Cat's best friend

Catnip is simply irresistible to cats. Fill a bag with catnip and watch your cat go crazy!

Catnip sock

Create a face on a colourful sock with buttons and beads and fill the sock with catnip. Add rice or dried peas to make it heavier. Tie a knot and let your cat loose on it.

Dried catnip

Herb wristband

Place some fresh herbs in a scarf, roll it up, and tie it into a knot. Take the lovely smells with you.

Try some rosemary, lavender, or mint.

Fold the scarf, roll it up, and tie it in a knot.

Wear it on your wrist

Smelly bundles

The smell of lavender helps you to sleep and also makes a room smell nice. Try making your own herb pouch. Place some lavender in a scarf, tie it up with an elastic band, and add a ribbon for decoration.

Fresh herb bundle

Elastic band

Lavender bundle

Fill the pot half way with compost.

Take the plants out of their small pots, position them, then fill up the gaps with compost.

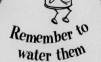

Remember to water them

35

Picture Pots

Give your plants a personality by decorating their pots.

Give me a makeover

Potted Gifts

Painted pots make perfect gifts. But why not take them a step further and paint the drip tray too? Put a gift in the pot, pop on the drip tray lid, and tie it up with a ribbon.

Sunflower fun

Beware! Magic seeds

 I make the perfect gift!

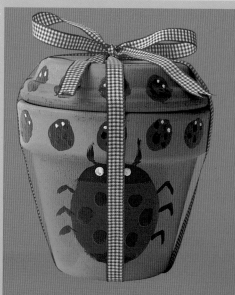

Bug alert!

Springtime gifts

In late summer, bulbs will start to appear in the shops. These can be planted straight away, ready to flower through the spring. The bulbs shown here are Narcissus bulbs called "Tête à Tête", they produce small flowers that are very perfumed.

How to grow them:

1. Lay gravel in the base of a 12 cm (5 in) pot.
2. Half fill the pot with compost.
3. Lay the bulbs on the surface of the soil.
4. Cover the bulbs with compost, and water.
5. Leave the pot in a dark place for about six weeks until the shoots appear – keep checking them.
6. Then bring them out into the light, keep them watered, and watch them grow.

After about eight weeks, the bulbs are ready to be given away

Perfect presents

If you are giving the bulbs away as a gift, put the drip tray on the top and tie the whole thing up in a spring ribbon.

Tie this up with a ribbon or paint it first

D.I.Y. gift kits

An alternative to planting the bulbs is to give away a DIY kit with all the ingredients necessary to grow them.

• SEED KITS – Give someone a pot and pop inside a packet of seeds and enough gravel and compost to plant a single pot. Sunflowers, annuals, herbs, pumpkins, or tomatoes are good gifts.

• BULB KITS – Include about five bulbs and enough gravel and compost inside a pot. Choose bulbs such as tulips, daffodils, hyacinth, or crocus.

• TOOL KITS – Give away a small fork, trowel, labels, gardening gloves, and plant ties.

These are called Narcissus "Tête à Tête"

How to Prepare Your Potted Gifts

Fill up your pot with all the goodies, place the drip tray on the top, and tie a ribbon around it.

Cross two ribbons in the middle.

1.

Make sure the ribbon is long enough to make a bow.

Ribbons and bows

Sit the pot in the centre of the crossed ribbons, tie one set of ribbons up first, then bring the other two ends up and tie them in a bow.

Whatever you do, don't turn the pot upside down!

Tie the first lengths of ribbon in a knot.

2.

Tie the second lengths in a bow.

Surprise surprise! Open it up and see what's inside

3.

This kit includes a packet of seeds, a bag of gravel and a bag of compost.

Add a painted pebble.

Flower Seeds

Allsorts

40

Thin and thick brushes

Mix up the paint

To paint pebbles and pots, use acrylic or poster paint. To make sure they are shiny and waterproof, mix the paints with PVA glue. Use one dollop of PVA to every two dollops of paint.

PVA glue

Acrylic or poster paint

How to paint pots, pebbles, and Ping-Pong balls

Paint a pot

You can paint both terracotta and plastic pots. Start by cleaning the pot to get rid of any dust or grit. Then mix up the paint with PVA glue and get designing. First try a simple pattern, then when you've got the hang of it, go decorating crazy!

PVA glue

Acrylic paint

Water

Paint straight onto the pot.

First paint the whole pot in one colour.

When the base colour is dry, start your designs.

Don't use the pot until it is totally dry.

Pebble pictures

Put the painted pebbles in your plant pots or hide them around the garden for people to find. Any shaped pebble will do. Clean off any grit and dirt, then decorate it with the paint and PVA mixture.

Hide us around the garden for visitors to find

Put the paint mixture on a clean pebble.

A pebble with your initial on it is a good label for your plants.

Ping-Pong ball plant labels

Fill your garden area with little signposts

Plant curious Ping-Pong labels all over your garden. Simply make a hole in a Ping-Pong ball and stick it on top of a plant cane. Use waterproof pens and paint to decorate them and write on the name of the plant. You could design a strange label that leaves people guessing what your plant is.

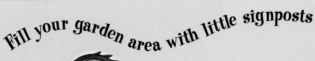

Give a tomato label some green leaves by making a hole for pipe cleaners.

Make a hole in the ball and push it on top of a stick.

Paint the sticks as well.

You could always write the name of the plant on the back to remind you what it is.

Roots and Shoots

Roots go down and shoots go up.

Let's see if beans know which way to grow.

Mixed beans

Try these any time of year

Bean machines

Place a selection of dried beans in a glass, fill the glass with water, and soak them overnight. Prepare another glass with damp kitchen paper wrapped around the inside. When your beans have finished soaking, carefully place them around the edge.

Which beans can you try?

Butter   Kidney   Cannellini   Black-eye   Haricot   Soy   Aduki

Make sure you cover the beans in water when you soak them.

Who won the race? Which bean is the fastest?

The bean case is still hanging on.

The race is on!

After about two days they will begin to sprout. Do the roots go down and shoots go up? What happens if you turn the bean upside down? Remember to keep them moist.

Keep the paper moist.

42

Mung beans

Mustard seeds

Cress seeds

Scatter the seeds and grow a field!

A good crop

Try having a go at growing wheat grains, these ones came from a local farm. The seed grows into wheat and then produces grain that is used to make bread. You could ask for whole wheat, rye, or barley. Soak the grains overnight in a glass and then simply lay them on damp kitchen paper. Keep it moist and watch your wheat field grow.

Soak the grains overnight before laying them on damp kitchen paper.

Check that the paper is moist everyday.

Weird Gardens

Welcome to the twilight world
of weird and wonderful plant life.

Plants that live on air, plants that live on meat, and plants that simply don't look like plants at all! The plant kingdom is a strange, strange world.

Air plants

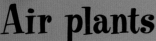

Imagine a plant that needs no soil, barely needs water, and doesn't even like too much sunlight. It's impossible, or is it? This is an air plant. They grow in Central America and because they do not root into the ground, they can perch on rocks, trees, and even telegraph wires! They hardly demand any attention, but will certainly attract it.

Hey! When will you need ME?

Chuck away your watering can! Pop the air plant in a vase or perch it on a surface and give it a good, all over spray, with cooled, boiled water about once a week.

Meat eaters

That's weird. A plant that eats meat? Introduce yourself to the Venus fly trap. This lethal carnivore eats any kind of insect that dares to fly near it. The insect is attracted to the plant's special scent, it then lands on it, and the fly trap quickly closes its deadly jaws. Leave these plants on a sunny windowsill and give them a lot of water to drink with their snacks.

Careful or you'll get eaten alive!

Flies just can't resist the smell.

Stand in 5 mm (1/8 in) of water.

Yum Yum!

What a strange looking plant!

Stick together this is getting strange

Watch where you put your feet

Living stones

They look like stones and if you put them with stones then no-one would know the difference. But these stones breathe. They are a kind of succulent, like a cactus, that live in hot, dry places. Plant them in suitable soil and then place stones around them. They should be kept in a dry place and watered every two weeks.

45

Growing Tips - Helpful hints for

Here are some useful things to know when you want to get started.

REMEMBER!

The essential things a plant must have are:

WATER
and
LIGHT

Plant names

When you are looking for a plant, it's worth remembering that they often have two names. This can be confusing. All plants have a Latin name, which is the same in every language throughout the world, and they also have a common name, which you and I would know them by. On a packet or label, you will almost always find both the common and the Latin name. Here are some examples:

Marigold – *Calendula*
Pumpkin – *Cucurbita pepo*
Lavender – *Lavandula vera*
Poppy – *Papaver*

As you can see, the common names are much easier to say!

Seed packets and plant labels

Read the information carefully on packets and labels that come with a plant. They will tell you:

• The common and the Latin name.
• When to sow seeds – the season or month.
• How large the plant will grow – height and width.
• How often to water it and when to feed it.
• When it is likely to flower.
• Any other instructions that are essential to healthy growth.

Plants need sunlight

Plants that are left in the dark will starve to death. Plants need food just like you do, but they make their own. They make energy from sunlight and use this energy to make a sugar called glucose. If they don't get sunlight, they will die.

Sunflower - Helianthus *or say in Latin*

Switching pots

When you need to re-pot the plants, such as squashes, be very careful as you do it. Tip the pot upside-down and gently ease out the plant, supporting the top. Place it in a bigger pot and fill around the edges with compost. Gently press down the soil and water it immediately.

When to water

You need to check on your plants about once a week to make sure they have enough water. Try using rain water rather than tap water, which has minerals added that are not kind to your plants. Plants do most of their growing in spring and summer so that's when it helps to add plant food to the water.

A spray each day keeps plants fresh

Spraying

Spraying can be done everyday, however, it is not strictly necessary. It keeps the plants fresh and damp.

The stone test

Stones around your plants aren't just there to look good, they can also tell you if your plant needs watering. Turn the stone over and:

• if it's damp = don't water.

• if it's dry = water now!

With most plants the soil should always be damp.

Plant food

It is good to add plant food or liquid fertilizer to your plant soil every so often. They give the plant vital nutrients and make sure the plant has everything it needs for healthy growth. Give it to them about once a week during its growing time.

Plant friends or foe?

There are some bugs that are kind to your plants and protect them, and some that just want to eat them. Greenfly are pests. The best thing to do if you find these little beasts is to look for a ladybird and bring it to the rescue. Ladybirds eat flies that want to eat your plants.

Be nice to bees, they are kind to your plants

One last thing:
BE PATIENT!
Plants take a while to grow, so enjoy the wait.

Index

Acknowledgements

With thanks to...
Maisie Armah, Charlotte Bull, Billy Bull,
James Bull, and Sorcha Lyons
for being budding gardeners.

Thanks to Paul Goff for the photography
of the "real" bonsai trees on pages12-13.

All images © Dorling Kindersley.
For further information see:
www.dkimages.com